JOE NAMATH

PHOTO CREDITS
All photos by Bruce Curtis
Published by Creative Educational Society, Inc.,
123 South Broad Street, Mankato, Minnesota 56001
Copyright © 1977 by Creative Educational Society, Inc. International
copyrights reserved in all countries.
No part of this book may be reproduced in any form without written
permission from the publisher. Printed in the United States.
Library of Congress Cataloging in Publication Data

Eldred, Patricia Mulrooney.
Football's great quarterback, Joe Namath.
1. Namath, Joe Willie, 1943-   —Juvenile
literature.   2. Quarterback (Football)—Biography—
Juvenile literature.   I. Title.
GV939:N28E4   796.33'2'0924 [B]   76-27359
ISBN 0-87191-580-4

FOOTBALL'S
GREAT QUARTERBACK
JOE NAMATH
BY PATRICIA MULROONEY ELDRED

CREATIVE EDUCATION/CHILDRENS PRESS

Joe Namath looks straight ahead. He grips the football firmly. His fingers are spread apart for control. His powerful arm is raised and ready to make the throw.

It all looks so simple. But the famous New York Jets quarterback spends hours practicing this same move before and during each football season. Joe doesn't mind the demands of his job because football is his life.

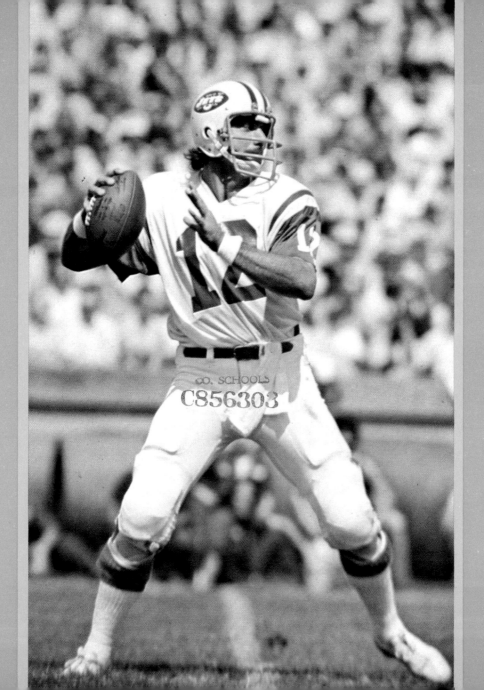

6

Joe learned to play football from his three older
brothers in Beaver Falls, Pennsylvania. "Throw from
your ear," the older boys used to shout to Joe. He
caught on quickly. And as he grew older passing
became his specialty.

Today, his opponents live in fear of Namath's
long bomb. One rival says, "If he has the slightest
amount of time, there is no real defense against him.
He'll get off a perfect pass."

8

Joe never looks rushed. Yet he moves quickly, shifting his weight from left to right as he cocks the ball. He knows he can be sacked at any moment. But he depends on his teammates and his own sense of timing for protection.

10

Spotting his receiver, Joe snaps his wrist and throws. As he releases the ball he twists his hips and shoulders. His body turns in almost a full circle. The style is unique. And it works. Most of the time Joe hits his target.

12

Joe Namath signed his first professional football contract in 1965. The agreement shocked Joe as much as it did everyone else. The Jets promised him a package worth almost half a million dollars. Joe was the first rookie in pro football to earn that much money. He liked the fame. He liked the money. He especially liked the Lincoln Continental convertible. His only other car had been a 1952 Ford with no doors. Joe was only 22 years old, and he felt that he was sitting on top of the world.

14

But the huge salary also created problems. The veteran players resented the young rookie. Joe discovered he had to gain the respect of his teammates. He had to show them how well he could play football. And he did.

At the end of Joe's first season he was named Rookie of the Year. He was proud to be the only rookie on the AFL All-Star team. He was even prouder when he was picked as the Most Valuable Offensive Player in the All-Star game. It was a good beginning.

Joe's career has been packed with excitement. One of his favorite memories is of the 1969 Super Bowl game. Three days before the game Joe publicly predicted the outcome. "We're going to win. I guarantee it."

Many people thought he was a loud-mouth. No one expected the Jets to win that game. The Baltimore Colts were favored by 18 points. The Jets belonged to the American Football League, and no team in the AFL had won a Super Bowl game. But Joe had confidence in the Jets. He had watched films of the Colts, and he thought he knew their weaknesses.

18

On Super Bowl Sunday the spectators sat stunned. Again and again Joe threw the football toward George Sauer or Matt Snell. He completed 17 out of 28 passes, gaining 206 yards. The dynamic young quarterback skillfully picked apart the Colts' defense. When the game ended, the Jets were Number 1. The score — Jets 16, Colts, 7. And it was no surprise that Joe Namath was named the Most Valuable Player in the game.

20

Joe has always believed in doing his own thing. He grew long hair before most athletes did. He sometimes wore an expensive fur coat. One year he grew a Fu Manchu mustache and then earned $10,000 for shaving it off in a TV commercial. His white football shoes became a trademark soon after he joined the Jets.

Many people have objected to Joe's appearance and behavior. But Joe doesn't pay much attention to what people think. He has often said, "I believe in letting a guy live the way he wants to if he doesn't hurt anyone."

22

Joe's major concern is always football. Each touchdown pass he throws gives him a special thrill. "It's like your whole body's bursting with happiness," he says.

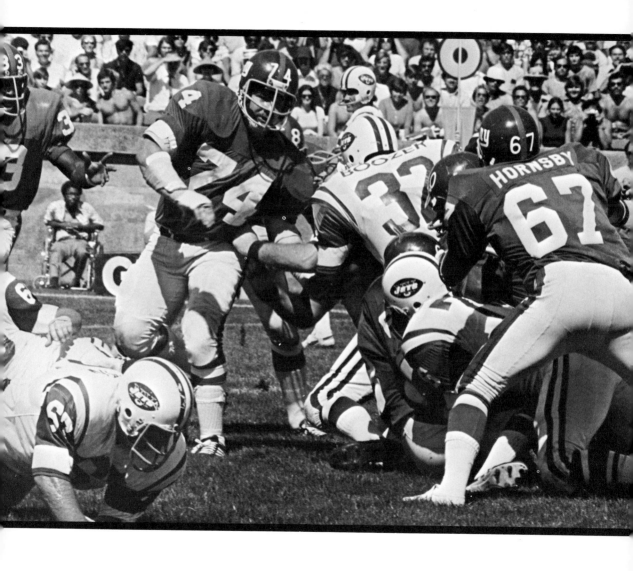

24

However, Joe has paid for his thrills with much pain. "Namath has the knees of a 70-year-old man," the Jets' doctor said in 1965. Since then Joe has had surgery several times. Today he must wear a metal brace on each knee when he plays. He often needs pain-killing injections before a game.

Joe's injuries have kept him out of many games. As a result he has not set many records. Yet many people still consider Joe Namath the best quarterback of all time.

26

Although Joe is often in pain, he ignores it when he plays football. He focuses his whole attention on the game. Before each play, Joe studies the field carefully. Sometimes he calls a play the coach has suggested. Other times he substitutes one of his own.

Joe's teammates have confidence in their quarterback. They seem to agree with one Jet coach who said, "Joe's football intelligence must be in the genius range."

28

Joe can almost always figure out an opposing team's plans. This amazes the fans and the opponents. Many times Joe calls a play from the line of scrimmage instead of in the huddle. "Unless I have some sort of mental lapse, I know what they're doing on defense every time," he says.

30

Like a magnet Joe draws huge crowds wherever he plays ball. And he obviously enjoys being a celebrity. He likes giving autographs, being recognized, shaking hands, talking with his fans.

But most of all Joe Namath likes playing football. As he says, "When you think you're the best at what you do you want to prove it."

BILLIE JEAN KING

O.J. SIMPSON

EVEL KNIEVEL

HANK AARON

JOE NAMATH

OLGA KORBUT

FRAN TARKENTON

MUHAMMAD ALI

CHRIS EVERT

FRANCO HARRIS

BOBBY ORR

KAREEM ABDUL JABBAR

JACK NICKLAUS

JOHNNY BENCH

JIMMY CONNERS

A.J. FOYT

THE ALLSTARS